SCIENTIFIC
BREAKTHROUGHS

DISCOVERIES IN
CHEMISTRY
that changed the world

Rose Johnson

rosen publishing's
rosen
central

Published in 2015 by The Rosen Publishing Group, Inc.
29 East 21st Street, New York, NY 10010

© 2015 Brown Bear Books Ltd

First Edition

Library of Congress Cataloging-in-Publication Data
Johnson, Rose, 1981-
 Discoveries in chemistry that changed the world / Rose Johnson.
    pages cm. -- (Scientific breakthroughs)
 Audience: Grades 5-8.
 Includes bibliographical references and index.
 ISBN 978-1-4777-8605-5 (library bound)
1. Discoveries in science--History. 2. Chemistry--History. 3. Chemistry--Study and teaching (Elementary) 4. Chemistry--Study and teaching (Middle school) I. Title.
 QD40.J625 2015
 540--dc23

                           2014025362

Editor and Text: Rose Johnson
Editorial Director: Lindsey Lowe
Children's Publisher: Anne O'Daly
Design Manager: Keith Davis
Designers: Lynne Lennon and Jeni Child
Picture Researcher: Clare Newman
Picture Manager: Sophie Mortimer

Brown Bear Boo ks has made every attempt to contact the copyright holder. If anyone has any information please contact:
licensing@brownbearbooks.co.uk

All artwork: © Brown Bear Books

Manufactured in Malaysia

Contents

Introduction

> Chemistry is the science that studies substances. It tries to figure out what things are made of and how they can be transformed into new substances.

We may not realize it, but humans have been studying chemistry for thousands of years. Lighting fires, making bread, turning clay into pottery, and purifying metals all involve chemical processes, called reactions.

Simple view

In ancient times, people thought that the world was made up of just four basic ingredients called elements. They were earth, fire, water, and air. It was believed that all natural processes, such as wind, rain, and volcanoes, were driven by these four elements all

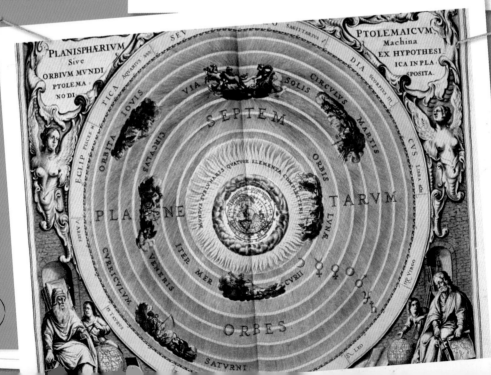

A map of the universe drawn by the ancient Greek philosopher Ptolemy shows rings made up of the different elements.

Purified hot iron pours into a mold. Making iron and other pure metals is part of chemistry.

trying to separate out from each other into layers. The lowest layer was made of cold and heavy earth (and rock). The next layer was water, then air, and at the very top—just before you got to the Moon—was a ring of fire.

From wizards to wisdom

The world really is made from elements, and there are 92 natural ones. Many of them were discovered by alchemists. Alchemists were not scientists. They believed that chemical reactions involved magic, and if they could figure it out they could live forever and be fabulously wealthy. We get the word "chemistry" from alchemist, and chemists still use some of the alchemists' techniques. The difference is that chemistry has succeeded in revealing how matter works.

Every substance on Earth is made up of combinations of 92 basic ingredients, such as sulfur (shown below).

5

Atoms

All the substances we find on Earth are made up of building blocks called atoms. This is actually a very ancient idea, first thought up by Greek philosophers.

About 2,400 years ago, Democritus came up with a theory of atoms that fits quite closely with our modern understanding.

T he idea of atoms was developed by two philosophers, Leucippus of Miletus (400s BCE) and his student, Democritus (c460–370 BCE), who lived in Turkey in the 5th century BCE. Their idea for atoms came from the suggestion that the world was in fact an illusion.

Chasing a tortoise

Another Greek called Xeno told the story of Achilles (a great warrior) chasing a tortoise. Every time Achilles halved the distance between himself and the tortoise, the reptile had crawled on a little bit. So, said Xeno, Achilles always got closer but could never catch up.

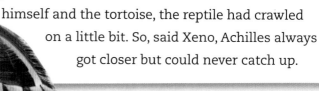

According to the Greek philosophers, if the world did not have atoms, a tortoise could outrun a human—or at least appear to.

Indivisible units

Xeno used his story to suggest that motion was actually impossible. Every distance had to be covered in an infinite number of steps—you would travel forever and never get anywhere. In response Leucippus suggested that the universe was made from tiny units that were the smallest size possible—so small they could not be halved. He called them atoms, which means indivisible.

Properties of matter

Democritus used this idea of atoms to describe the properties of natural substances: The atoms of water were slippery, fire atoms were spiky, while earth was made from sticky atoms that clung together. Although atoms are more complicated than this, centuries later, scientists found that everything is made from atoms.

In the days of Democritus, it was thought everything was made of just four elements: air, fire, water and earth.

FACTS

● Democritus is known as the Laughing Philosopher. He thought the universe had no purpose and so it was best to just be happy.
● There are 90 types of atoms that occur naturally on Earth and several more that are made in laboratories.

Discovering Elements

The basic substances studied by chemistry are the elements. Scientists have discovered 118 of them so far. The first recorded discovery was in 1669.

IMPLICATIONS

Phosphorus is very useful. It is added to the fertilizers that help crops grow. It is also one of the chemicals used in matches, which make it possible to create fire anywhere.

An element is a substance that cannot be broken into any simpler ingredients. Ancient people believed the Universe was made from just four or five elements, but by the 17th century it was understood there were actually many more. Substances like carbon, gold, iron, copper, and sulfur were being classed as elements as well.

Getting rich quick

The people who studied elements at this time were called alchemists. They were more like wizards than scientists.

Rubbing these matches on a rough surface makes phosphorus in the head burst into flames.

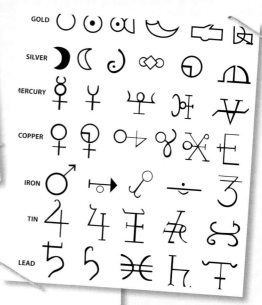

When Hennig Brand saw that phosphorus glowed, he thought he had discovered a magical substance.

GOLD

SILVER

MERCURY

COPPER

IRON

TIN

LEAD

They were searching for magical substances that could make them live forever and turn any substance into gold.

Boiling down

In 1669, a German alchemist called Hennig Brand (1630–1710) wanted to see if he could make gold from urine—they were the same color after all! He boiled down a huge vat of urine and experimented with the crystals and oils that were left behind. He eventually produced a small amount of liquid that glowed in the dark! He called this phosphorus, which means "light giver." Phosphorus is a common element in nature and our bodies. Brand was the first known person to have discovered an element. The most recent element to be discovered is ununseptium. It was officially confirmed in 2014.

The symbols alchemists used for substances are now associated with wizards and witchcraft.

Studying "Airs"

Modern chemistry began in the 18th century, when scientists began to investigate the behavior of different "airs"—what we would now call gases.

U ntil well into the 18th century, scientists followed the teachings of ancient Greek philosophers who said that the main elements in nature were earth (or rock), fire, water, and air. It was thought that natural substances were a mixture of these four elements. For example, coal was seen as a mixture of fire, earth, and air. When it burned, these three elements separated out forming flames, smoke, and ash.

A new approach

In the 1660s, the Irish scientist Robert Boyle (1627–1691) began to study the properties of air using a scientific approach. Unlike the alchemists of the past, he did not believe that

The bubbles in soda are carbon dioxide. This gas was the first one to be identified as a substance separate from air.

Joseph Black (seated right) was an expert on gases and heat. He is seen here discussing them with James Watt (standing center), who developed high-powered steam engines.

magic had anything to do with understanding nature. Boyle used a pump to suck the air out of flasks. He made many discoveries, including the fact that air pressure was inversely proportional to its volume. In other words, the pressure of air went up as it was made to fill a smaller and smaller container. This suggested that the gas was filled with invisible units that pushed against the container walls, creating the pressure force.

Carbon dioxide

Boyle thought that air was an element, just a single, pure substance. However, Scottish doctor Joseph Black (1728–1799) found that it was really a mixture of different "airs." In the 1750s, Black discovered "fixed air," which we now call carbon dioxide. Black made his discovery as he studied magnesia alba, a white mineral used in

Hydrogen is a very light gas. Hydrogen balloons were first used as flying machines in 1783. This one was used in the American Civil War (1861–1865) to spy on the enemy.

FACTS

- The word gas replaced "air" in the 1800s. It was based on the word "chaos."
- The most common gas on Earth is nitrogen.
- Only 11 out of 118 known elements are gases in everyday conditions.

medicines. He found that he could make the crystals give off an invisible air. He then showed that animals breathed out the same substance. Finally, he found that if an animal was put inside a jar of "fixed air," it died.

Hydrogen

The next air, or gas, was discovered in 1766. A century before that Robert Boyle had found that when metal was put in strong acids it gave off bubbles of "air" that burned easily. Boyle thought this was just very pure air. However, English scientist Henry Cavendish (1731–1810) figured out that it was a separate gas. He called it "flammable air," but today it is named hydrogen.

Nitrogen

In 1772, another English scientist, Daniel Rutherford (1749–1819), investigated what other gases might be in air. He knew that burning a candle inside a glass jar increased the amount of fixed air (carbon dioxide) inside. He then filtered out all the "fixed air," but found the gas left behind was still not good to breathe. He had discovered that most of the air is made of a different gas, which we now call nitrogen.

Oxygen

Nothing burns in nitrogen. Flames just go out. In 1774, the English researcher Joseph Priestley found a gas that made flames more powerful. He produced it by heating a chemical containing mercury. The process gave off the gas that we now call oxygen. Later, scientists would reveal how oxygen is involved in burning.

JOSEPH PRIESTLEY

Joseph Priestley was born in Yorkshire, England, in 1733. As well as being one of the discoverers of oxygen (a Swede called Carl Scheele also found it around the same time), Priestley invented soda water in 1770. In 1794, he moved to the United States, where he discovered the gas carbon monoxide. He died in Pennsylvania in 1804.

A scuba diver breathes from a tank filled with a mixture of nitrogen and oxygen.

Combustion

Although people had been using fire for more than 100,000 years, no one understood what it was until the work of the great French chemist, Antoine Lavoisier.

Combustion is the scientific name for burning. Burning releases heat and light, and substances that burn easily are called fuels. For thousands of years, people had used fuels for cooking food, keeping warm, and for firing pottery and purifying metals. However, in the 18th century fuels were also becoming important for powering machines, like steam locomotives.

Phlogiston

An early scientific theory of burning said that fuels contained a substance called phlogiston. During

Flames are curious things. They are made of super hot gases that have been heated up by the energy given out by combustion.

Lavoisier showed that when things burned they were reacting with oxygen gas in the air.

burning, the fuels released the phlogiston, which traveled through the air and was felt by the body as heat. Early chemists used this idea to understand the properties of gases (or "airs"). Nitrogen did not allow burning and so it was said to be "phlogisticated"—it was completely full of phlogiston, and so burning stopped. By contrast, an early name for oxygen was "dephlogisticated air." That meant it had no phlogiston in it and so made burning faster as it sucked in this substance.

Using oxygen

Many scientists had noted that when metals burned (or heated to red hot) they became heavier. It did not make sense that something got heavier after losing phlogiston. In the 1770s, Antoine Lavoisier showed that burning was a chemical reaction, where two substances combined to form a new substance and released heat as they did so. The burning reaction always involved oxygen, the newly discovered gas.

Fire needs oxygen, so firefighters smother the flames with foam. This blocks the supply of oxygen and stops the burning.

Water former

It was Lavoisier who gave oxygen its name. The word means "acid former." Lavoisier was wrong that oxygen has anything to do with acids, but the name stuck. He also came up with the name hydrogen, which means "water former." Like several earlier chemists, Lavoisier noticed that after hydrogen gas was burned inside a flask, droplets of water formed on the inside. Back then water was thought to be an element, a simple substance that was not made up of other ingredients. Lavoisier showed that water was actually made from a combination of hydrogen and oxygen. The two gases were joined together during burning, or combustion.

ANTOINE LAVOISIER

Born in Paris, France, in 1743, Antoine Lavoisier's family worked for the French king. In 1789, the French people rose up against the king. The new government asked Lavoisier to help set up a fairer system of measurements (later named the metric system). Nevertheless, in 1794, Lavoisier was executed for his family's links to the old royal government.

Same weights

Lavoisier showed that the weight of substances involved in chemical reactions, including combustion, did not change. So the weight of water (and steam) produced by burning hydrogen and oxygen was always the same as the weight of the two starting gases. This rule, known as the conservation of matter, is central to the modern understanding of chemistry.

Breathe in and out

Lavoisier also showed that animal bodies are powered by the combustion of food. The body takes in oxygen and gives out carbon dioxide and water vapor. These two gases are produced when food is simply burned in oxygen.

IMPLICATIONS

Lavoisier was a very important figure in chemistry. He came up with the system for naming chemicals after the elements they contained, such as iron oxide, copper sulfate, and nitric acid. He also drew up one of the first scientific lists of elements, or "simple substances," as he called them, which would later become the periodic table.

The gases in an animal's breath show that its body is burning food in a similar process to the way an engine burns fuel.

17

Atomic Theory

The study of gases led to one of the greatest discoveries in chemistry. In 1803, the scientist John Dalton showed that everything is made from atoms.

The idea of atoms was a very old one. It had been put forward in the 5th century BCE by the Greek philosopher Democritus and others. However, none of them had put forward any evidence for atoms. To them it was just an idea. Later scientists had tried to explain natural processes in terms of invisible units called "corpuscles" or "molecules," but the first theory of atoms backed up by scientific observations was set out by the English scientist John Dalton in 1803.

Mixture of gases

Dalton's theory came from his hobby of recording the weather. Every day he recorded the temperature and air pressure. This gave

Colored liquids diffuse in water. All fluids—gases and liquids—do this. The atoms and molecules are in constant motion and naturally spread out from each other.

John Dalton's atomic theory became the foundation of how we understand chemistry today.

him an idea about how gases behaved. Air was a mixture of gases, which worked together to produce a single value for air pressure (the force of the gases pushing on other objects). Dalton figured out that each gas in the mixture contributed a fraction of the total pressure.

Diffusion

Dalton knew that a gas diffuses, which means it spreads out to fill any container. He realized that mixed gases diffuse independently. Equal amounts of two gases in a bottle will spread to all parts of the container, so wherever you look you will find a mixture made of half of one gas and half of the other—each one creating half of the total pressure.

JOHN DALTON

John Dalton was born in 1766 and spent most of his life in Manchester, England. He was the tutor of James Joule, who later made discoveries about how energy and heat work. Dalton was color blind and was the first person to describe this condition. He died in Manchester in 1844.

Different units

John Dalton put these two ideas together. Even when mixed with others, a substance stays separate from those around it and maintains its unique set of physical properties. To do that, Dalton reasoned, substances must be made up of tiny but distinct units. He chose the ancient word "atom" to describe them.

Indestructible

Dalton also looked at the chemical properties of mixed gases—how they reacted with each other. He knew that substances combined in fixed ratios, and the total weight of material before a reaction was the same as after it. So the atoms never changed weight and could not be created or destroyed.

Dalton's diagrams were the first realistic explanation of how atoms combine to produce different substances.

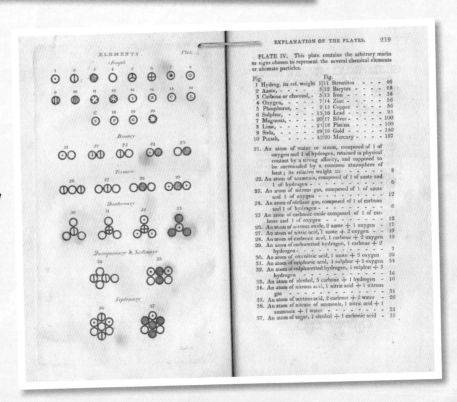

These tanks are filled with carbon dioxide. The formula shows that one atom of carbon (C) bonds to two of oxygen (O).

Chemical combinations

The view of atoms Dalton built up was of little solid spheres. However, he also knew that these balls could cluster together. When the atoms of two or more elements joined together they made units of an entirely different material—like hydrogen and oxygen make water. He imagined that the atoms clustered together in the same ratios as they combined on the large scale. He drew diagrams of these atom clusters, which in modern terms are described as molecules.

Atomic weights

Finally, Dalton saw that the atoms of different elements had a unique weight. Hydrogen atoms were the lightest, and Dalton listed elements according to their atomic weight. This is still how elements are ordered today.

Iron becomes rust when the metal's atoms combine with atoms of oxygen and hydrogen.

21

Electrolysis

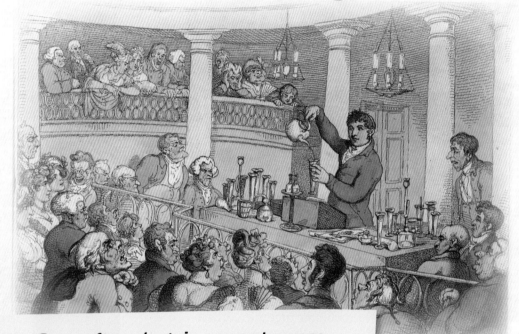

Soon after electric currents were discovered, chemists were using them to split substances apart.

Humphry Davy was famous for giving science lectures to the public.

Many chemical reactions give out energy as heat and light. At the end of the 18th century, scientists found that they could make reactions run backward by adding energy with electricity. For example, hydrogen and oxygen burn together to make water. In 1800, scientists showed that when an electric current is run through water, the liquid turns back into the two gases. They found there was twice as much hydrogen (H) as oxygen (O), which showed that the formula for water was H_2O.

Making a battery

The first device for making electricity was called a pile. It was a pile of metal discs that created an electric current as they reacted. Many piles working together was known as a battery—named for a battery of guns. In 1807, an English scientist named Humphry Davy (1778–1829) built a huge battery in London. He used it for the new science of electrolysis— which means "splitting with electricity."

Discovery spree

In three years, Davy used electrolysis to discover six elements, more than any other scientist. They were sodium, potassium, magnesium, barium, boron and chlorine gas. This last one was the first known halogen, a group of reactive non-metals.

IMPLICATIONS

Iron and copper are refined using chemical reactions, but this does not work for most elements. Electrolysis is used instead. Aluminum, magnesium, sodium, and chlorine are all refined in this way. Industrial electrolysis needs a lot of energy. The compounds being refined are heated to high temperatures so they melt. Then huge electric currents are run through the hot liquid to extract the elements.

All the aluminum we use, such as these rolls of foil, is purified using electrolysis.

Spectroscopy

Every element burns with a different color flame. Spectroscopy, study of these colors, has shown that the same elements exist all over the Universe.

An early spectrometer used a telescope to focus the light of a flame through a prism.

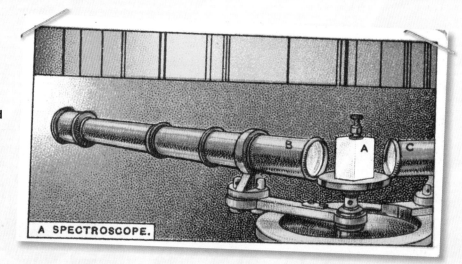

A SPECTROSCOPE.

One of the first things a chemist does when trying to figure out what a substance is made from is to set light to it. The color of the flame provides clues. For example, sodium burns with an orange flame, while potassium's flame is purple.

Famous burner

In 1855, a German chemist called Robert Bunsen (1811–1899) designed a gas burner that burned with a very clean flame. The Bunsen burner is now used as a source of heat in labs all over the world. However, Bunsen initially used it to study the colors of flames.

Prism system

Bunsen was joined by fellow German Gustav Kirchhoff (1824–1887) who used a prism to split the light from a flame into its separate colors. This apparatus, known as a spectrometer, showed that the flames were not a blend of colors, but were a set of very distinct beams of light. The scientists found that every element produced a unique set of these beams, known as its emission spectrum.

Light clues

Bunsen and Kirchhoff were able to identify new elements from the lights they gave off. In addition, when starlight was viewed through a spectrometer, it showed that the stars were made from elements just like those on Earth.

IMPLICATIONS

Investigating why elements produce specific colors of light led to an understanding about the structure of the atom. It was shown that the electrons inside atoms of different elements could only absorb and release light at specific wavelengths, or colors.

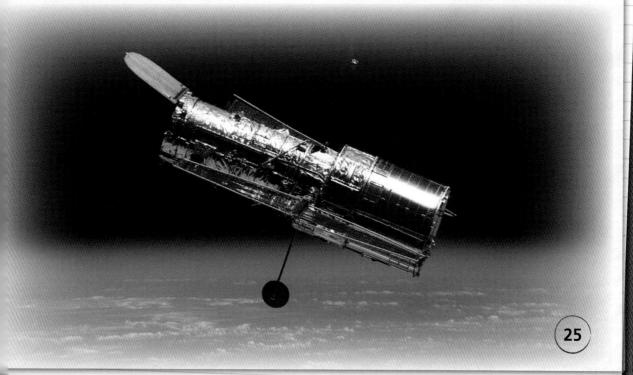

The Hubble Space Telescope uses a spectrometer to analyze the light coming from stars, clouds of gas, and other astronomical bodies.

25

Discovering Helium

The element helium was discovered by studying the light coming from the Sun. It was the first of the inert, or noble, gases to be discovered.

In 1868, two researchers working independently looked at the light coming from a solar eclipse using spectroscopes. Their devices split the light into its individual colors and they reported seeing a band of unusual yellow light. One of the two, the Englishman Norman Lockyer realized that the light was coming from a previously unknown element. He named it "helium," after "helios," the Greek word for "sun."

Evidence of helium was discovered in the ring of light that surrounds the Sun during a solar eclipse.

Unreactive

In 1895, a sample of helium was isolated for the first time by the Scottish chemist William Ramsay (1852–1916). He found it to be an inert gas—he could not make it react with any other element. Ramsay also found a similar gas mixed into the air. He named it argon. By 1898, Ramsay had found three more: neon, krypton, and xenon.

Noble gases

The elements were named the noble gases, meaning they did not mix with the more common elements. The group would later provide a valuable clue as to how the structure of atoms controlled an element's properties.

Tubes of noble gas glow when electrified. They are often called neon lights, although other gases are used as well.

IMPLICATIONS

Helium has the lowest melting point of any element. It only becomes solid at −458 °F (−272°C). When researchers cooled helium to near these temperatures they found it became a superfluid. This is an amazing material that cannot be stored in a container—it flows up the sides and escapes!

Periodic Table

In 1869, Dmitri Mendeleev came up with a new way of organizing the elements. His periodic table is still used in chemistry laboratories around the world.

Chemists have been trying to figure out a way of organizing the elements since the days of the alchemists. The most obvious system was to list elements according to the weight of their atoms. (This value is now described as an element's atomic mass.) Chemists already knew that every element had a unique atomic mass. The problem was that atoms are so small it is impossible to count them. That made it very difficult to figure out how much each one weighed.

DMITRI MENDELEEV

Born in Tobolsk, Siberia, in eastern Russia in 1834, Dmitri Mendeleev became a student of the great chemist Robert Bunsen. He developed the periodic table while a professor in St. Petersburg, Russia. He died in 1907, and in 1955 element 101 was named mendelevium in his honor.

It is said that Dmitri Mendeleev got the idea for the periodic table while playing Solitaire, a game where cards are arranged in rows.

	Gruppe I.	Gruppe II.	Gruppe III.	Gruppe IV.	Gruppe V.	Gruppe VI.	Gruppe VII.	Gruppe VIII.
Typische Elemente	H 1 Li 7	Be 9,4	Bo 11	C 12	N 14	O 16	F 19	
Reihe 1	Na 23	Mg 24	Al 27,3	Si 28	P 31	S 32	Cl 35,5	
- 2	Ka 39	Ca 40	—44	Ti 50(?)	V 51	Cr 52	Mn 55	Fe 56, Co 59, Ni 56, Cu [63
Reihe 3	(Cu 63)	Zn 65	—68	—72	As 75	Se 78	Br 80	
- 4	Rb 85	Sr 87	(Yt 88) (?)	Zr 90	Nb 94	Mo 96	—100	Ru 104, Rh 104, Pl 106, [Ag 108
Reihe 5	(Ag 108)	Cd 112	In 113	Sn 118	Sb 122	Te 125	J 127	
- 6	Cs 133	Ba 137	—137	Ce 138 (?)	—	—	—	
Reihe 7	—	—	—	—				
- 8	—	—	—	—	Ta 183	W 184	—	Os 199 (?), Jr 198, Pt [197, Au 197
Reihe 9	(Au 197)	Hg 200	Tl 204	Pb 207	Bi 208	—	—	
- 10	—	—	—	Th 232	—	Ur 240	—	
Höchste salz-bild. Oxyde	R^2O	R^2O^2 od. RO	R^2O^3	R^2O^4 o. RO^2	R^2O^5	R^2O^6 o. RO^3	R^2O^7	R^2O^8 od. RO^4
Höchste H-Verbindung				RH^4	RH^3	RH^2	RH	(R^2H) (?)

Left margin: 1. Periode 2. Periode 3. Periode 4. Periode 5. Periode

Mendeleev's first attempt at the periodic table left gaps for the many elements that had yet to be discovered.

Counting gas

In 1860, a meeting of chemists was held in Germany. There, the scientists figured out a way of measuring atomic masses. They knew that the pressure exerted by a gas was due to its atoms hitting the walls of its container. Therefore the pressure went up when more atoms were squeezed inside. That meant a fixed volume of gas at a fixed pressure and temperature always contained the same number of atoms. It did not matter what the gas was.

Comparing weights

Hydrogen was the lightest element and was given an atomic mass of 1. The same volume of oxygen weighed 16 times as much, and so it had an atomic mass of 16. This system was the first step in chemists figuring out an atomic mass for all elements. New elements were being discovered all the time. By 1869 there were 64.

Making rows

Dmitri Mendeleev's periodic table does more than list the elements according to atomic mass. It also groups elements that have the same chemical properties. The atoms of different elements have a limit to how many bonds they can make with other atoms. For example, sodium atoms only form one bond, carbon atoms can form four, while helium does not form any bonds at all. Mendeleev set out the elements in rows (or periods) in order of atomic mass. He also grouped elements with the same bond number in columns. This "periodic table" of elements proved to be a powerful tool.

The modern table shows the 118 elements in 18 columns, or groups, and seven periods. The last two periods are very wide so a section is shown along the bottom.

Non-metals like carbon (diamond) are on the right of the table. Metals make up the center and left. Semimetals, such as silicon, sit in between.

Atomic structure

Mendeleev did not realize it at the time but his table arranged elements according to how their atoms were organized. Atomic mass is produced by particles called protons and neutrons at the center of the atom. A hydrogen atom has one, while an oxygen has 16 particles. The number of bonds an atom forms depends on the electrons it has. Electrons are tiny particles that swirl around the atom. All the elements in a group (or column) have the same number of electrons in the outermost layer of their atoms.

At a glance

Mendeleev had some gaps in his version of the table. However, he used the table to predict what the element for each gap would be like. He was always proved right. Chemists can tell what kind of properties an element will have by where it sits in the periodic table.

Activation Energy

Most chemical reactions do not happen on their own. They need an input of energy, like heat, to get going. This is known as activation energy.

It was the Swedish chemist, Svante Arrhenius (1859–1927), who first proposed the idea that there was an energy barrier preventing reactions from occurring. The reactants (or starting materials) only reacted and recombined into a product if they had enough energy to get over this barrier. This theory helped scientists understand what was going on during chemical reactions.

IMPLICATIONS

A catalyst is a substance that reduces the activation energy needed for a reaction to take place. The catalyst is not used up by the reaction. A catalytic converter in a car uses platinum as a catalyst to turn poisonous gases in the exhaust into safer ones.

Catalytic converters in cars use chemical reactions to clean the pollution from exhaust gases.

A firework needs to be lit to start the chemical reactions that produce the lights and colors.

Breaking and making

During a chemical reaction, the atoms in the reactants are reorganized to make the product of the reaction. The activation energy is needed to break the bonds that keep the reactants together. Once their bonds are broken, the atoms will make new bonds with different atoms and form an entirely new substance.

Energy in and out

Heat energy is needed to break a chemical bond. However, when a new bond forms heat is given out. It is common for a reaction to give out more heat than it takes in, so the reaction produces flames and even explosions.

FACTS

- Svante Arrhenius also discovered the greenhouse effect. He calculated how adding carbon dioxide to the air would make the whole Earth warmer.
- Reactions speed up when substances are heated and put under high pressure.

33

Radioactivity

An accidental discovery in 1896 revealed a whole new area of chemistry. Some atoms are very unstable and break apart in a process called radioactivity.

Marie and Pierre Curie came up with the term "radioactivity" as they researched uranium.

French scientist Henri Becquerel (1852–1908) discovered radioactivity. He found it while looking to see if crystals that glowed in the dark gave out other invisible beams, such as X rays, which had been discovered in 1895. Becquerel covered photographic paper (this goes black when exposed to light) in thick card so no light could get in. He then put dozens of different crystals on top to see if any crystal sent a beam through and marked the paper.

MARIE CURIE

This Polish researcher is perhaps the most famous female scientist ever. She was born in Warsaw, and moved to Paris, France, in 1891 where she met her husband, Pierre. Both were awarded a Nobel Prize in 1903. Marie got a second one in 1911 (after Pierre had died), one of only four people to receive two.

FACTS

- The heat given out by natural radioactivity is what makes the center of Earth so hot.
- Power plants use the heat from uranium and other nuclear fuels to make electricity.
- Beams of radioactive radiation are used to burn away cancers inside the body.

Radiation of a different kind

All but one of the crystals had no effect. However, a yellow mineral called uranyl sulfate did mark the paper. This mineral contained uranium, and Becquerel found that other minerals containing uranium had the same effect. The radiation that these materials gave out did not behave like light waves. The mysterious effect was given the name "Becquerel rays."

More elements

Marie Curie (1867–1934) began to investigate the effect in uranium and discovered that thorium was also radioactive. (Marie made up this word by joining "radiation" and "active" together.) Working with her husband Pierre (1859–1906), she discovered two other radioactive elements, polonium and radium.

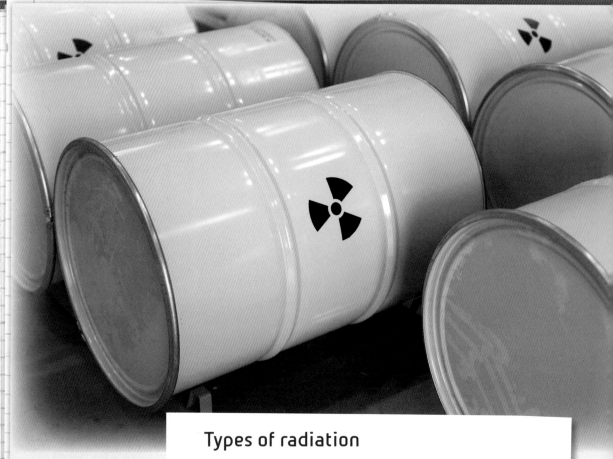

Radioactive material is used to make electricity and in medicine. However, the waste left behind must be stored in a safe place for hundreds —sometimes thousands—of years until it stops being dangerous.

Types of radiation

By 1900, other researchers had found that radioactive elements gave out three types of radiation, which were named with the first three letters of the Greek alphabet. Alpha radiation was made of particles that were positively charged, beta radiation was a beam of negatively charged particles, while gamma radiation were rays that behaved in the same way as light, radio waves, or heat, but carried huge amounts of energy.

Collapsing nucleus

Radioactivity is produced when the core, or nucleus of an atom is too unstable to hold itself together. As it collapses into a more stable arrangement, it fires out these three types of radiation. Most radioactive elements have very large atoms, which are more likely to be unstable. When a nucleus breaks up, or decays, it loses a bit of its atomic mass, and so the atom transforms into a new element. Highly radioactive elements decay away very quickly—they have a short half-life. The half-life is the time it takes for a half the sample to decay.

Danger!

All forms of radiation contain a large amount of energy. When they hit regular atoms, they knock bits off. That turns the atoms into charged ions, which can damage living tissue, causing illnesses, such as cancer. Today, radioactive material is treated with extreme care and stored in safe containers.

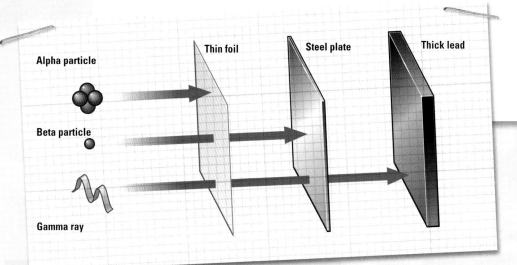

Alpha particle

Beta particle

Gamma ray

Thin foil

Steel plate

Thick lead

IMPLICATIONS

Radioactivity was an important tool in figuring out how atoms are structured from tiny subatomic particles. Scientists now know that an alpha particle is really a cluster of four particles—two protons and two neutrons. A beta particle is normally an electron, which is a much smaller subatomic particle.

Alpha particles are too big to get through foil. Beta particles are blocked by steel, but gamma rays are only stopped by thick shielding made from lead.

37

The Haber Process

Nitrogen is included in many useful chemicals. The Haber process made it possible to make a nitrogen compound called ammonia on a huge scale.

Nitrogen is an essential component in all living things. It is chiefly used to make the proteins that are at work in every aspect of the body. There is a natural nitrogen cycle, in which nitrogen from the air is converted into nitrates, where each nitrogen atom is bonded to three oxygens. Nitrates in the soil are essential for the growth of plants—and for the animals that feed on them. Nitrogen-containing chemicals are also used in many technologies, such as explosives and dyes.

FACTS

- Fritz Haber was awarded the Nobel Prize for his discovery.
- Before the Haber process one of the best sources of nitrates was guano, or bird droppings.
- Three percent of the world's energy supply is used to make ammonia.

Unreactive gas

Nitrogen is the most common gas on Earth—it makes up 70 percent of the air. However, it is not very reactive. Before 1911 no one knew how to make nitrogen compounds on a large scale. Instead, people mined natural sources of nitrate, but they were running out.

Chemical process

German chemist Fritz Haber (1868–1934) invented a process that reacted nitrogen from the air with hydrogen gas. That formed ammonia. This is a toxic gas, but it could be converted into more useful substances, such as fertilizers, nitric acid, plastics, and explosives, such as gunpowder and TNT. The world produces about 143 million tons (130 million tonnes) of ammonia every year.

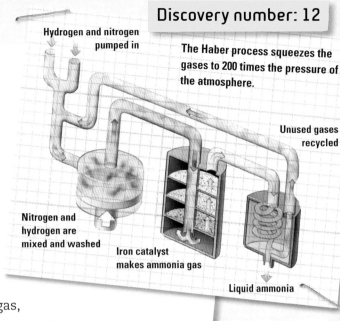

Hydrogen and nitrogen pumped in

The Haber process squeezes the gases to 200 times the pressure of the atmosphere.

Unused gases recycled

Nitrogen and hydrogen are mixed and washed

Iron catalyst makes ammonia gas

Liquid ammonia

Fertilizers sprayed onto crops are all produced by the Haber process.

IMPLICATIONS

The Haber process had a huge impact. Without it, World War I (1914–1918) would have been over in months because Germany would have run out of explosives. On a more positive note, approximately half of the world's people avoid starvation thanks to nitrogen-rich fertilizers.

Isotopes

1913, Frederick Soddy

The atoms of an element have a unique number of protons and electrons. The number of neutrons can vary, creating versions of atoms called isotopes.

All atoms have a nucleus surrounded by electrons. The nucleus is positively charged due to the presence of particles called protons. An element is defined by the number of protons it has in its nucleus. This is termed its atomic number. Hydrogen's atomic number is one, carbon's is six, while uranium's is 92. The number of electrons, which are negatively charged, equals the atomic number.

Extra weight

Electrons are so tiny that they are not counted when weighing an atom, but only hydrogen atoms have an atomic mass that equals its atomic number. All other elements have

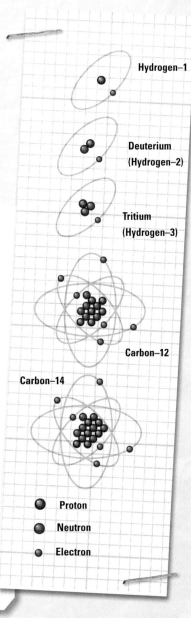

Hydrogen–1

Deuterium
(Hydrogen–2)

Tritium
(Hydrogen–3)

Carbon–12

Carbon–14

- ● Proton
- ● Neutron
- ● Electron

Hydrogen has three isotopes. Only hydrogen–1 is stable. Carbon–14 is a radioactive form of carbon.

Radiocarbon dating can tell us how old this Egyptian mummy is to within a few decades.

IMPLICATIONS

All living things contain carbon, and when they are alive that includes a tiny proportion of radioactive carbon-14. Once they die the amount of carbon-14 begins to fall as the isotope decays away. The amount of carbon-14 left tells us how old something is. Radiocarbon dating is used to date wood, cloth... and dead bodies!

extra particles in the nucleus, which add to the weight. These are neutrons. They weigh about the same as a proton but have no charge. The atomic mass of an element is the number of protons plus neutrons. Carbon's atomic mass is 12; iron's is 56.

Tiny variations

In 1913, the English chemist Frederick Soddy (1877–1956) showed that the atoms of an element could have slightly different masses. He called these different versions isotopes. The difference is due to a varying number of neutrons. Most elements have one main isotope, and any others are unstable and radioactive.

Transuranium Elements

Uranium is the heaviest element that exists in nature. However, it is possible to make larger atoms in laboratories.

U ranium and all the other heavy elements are highly radioactive. None of them have a stable isotope. That means that the amount of uranium is gradually going down. It is thought that half of it has disappeared since Earth was formed. It is likely that when Earth was much younger, even larger and more unstable elements than uranium existed, but they have all disappeared now.

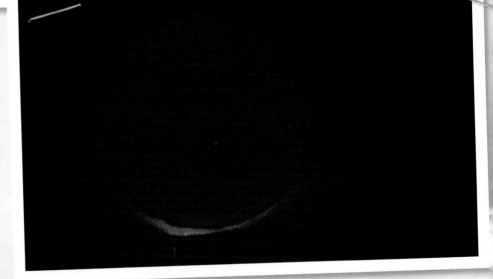

Plutonium, element 94, was one of the first transuranium elements. This sample is so radioactive that it glows red hot.

A tiny amount of the transuranium element americium is used in smoke alarms.

Atom smasher

In the 1940s, scientists around the world began to recreate some of these larger, transuranium elements. (Transuranium means "beyond uranium.") They did this by bombarding heavy elements, such as uranium and thorium, with beams of high-speed particles. Occasionally, the beams would be absorbed by a nucleus and its atomic number went up. It was a slow process, but gradually new elements were produced.

New discoveries

So far 26 transuranium atoms have been created. Many are named after famous scientists, like Marie Curie or Albert Einstein. The American scientist, Glenn Seaborg (1912–1999) made one of the first, the metal plutonium, in 1940. Seaborg went on to produce nine others, more than any other person. In 1997, element 106 was named seaborgium in his honor.

IMPLICATIONS

Many of the transuranium elements are so unstable that their samples only exist for a few minutes. However, scientists believe that even larger atoms would be more stable. If they can figure out how to make these substances they might have unimaginable properties.

43

Buckyballs

Carbon is a very special element. Its atoms can bond into many shapes and make everything from tough diamonds and slippery soot to balls and tubes.

The buckyball is named for Richard Buckminster Fuller. It shares the same structure as the domes Fuller designed in the 1950s.

It is possible for elements to exist in more than one form. Pure carbon can be diamond—a crystal that is the hardest substance in nature. Or it can be graphite, a grey solid that is very slippery.

Many shapes

Diamond and graphite are allotropes. It used to be thought that there was just one more allotrope of carbon. This was soot or charcoal in which the carbon atoms are all jumbled. By contrast, in diamond the atoms are arranged in a sturdy network of triangular-based pyramids. In graphite the carbons are arranged in sheets of hexagons stacked on top of each other. Each sheet is very strong—

1985 Curl, Kroto, and Smalley

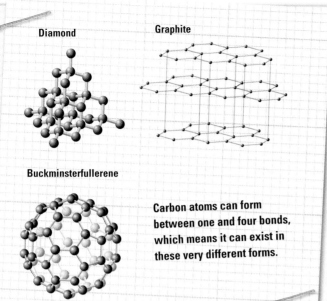

Diamond

Graphite

Buckminsterfullerene

Carbon atoms can form between one and four bonds, which means it can exist in these very different forms.

FACTS

- Nanotubes are so thin that if you rolled up a tube long enough to run from Earth to the Moon, it would only be the size of a poppy seed.
- Graphite is pencil "lead." A pencil mark is a layer of graphite on paper.
- When buckminsterfullerene is dissolved in oil it makes the mixture turn purple.
- Nanotubes are the strongest material ever discovered, hundreds of time stronger than steel.

when isolated it is known as graphene—but the layers are barely connected and slide around easily.

Balls and tubes

In 1985, Robert Curl, Harold Kroto, and Richard Smalley found that carbon could also form balls of 60 atoms. They named it buckminsterfullerene after a famous architect. The "buckyballs" could be extended to form long cylinders called nanotubes. These amazing substances might one day be used to build tiny machines.

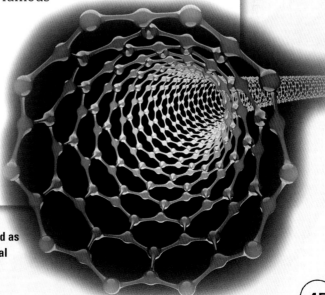

A nanotube could be used as a tiny pipe or an electrical wire—or both!

TIMELINE

1669: Hennig Brand discovers phosphorus. He is the first person known to have discovered a new element.

1750: Joseph Black discovers carbon dioxide gas.

1766: Henry Cavendish discovers hydrogen gas.

1772: Daniel Rutherford discovers nitrogen gas.

1774: Joseph Priestley finds oxygen. (Carl Scheele found it in 1772 but did not tell anyone.)

1775: Antoine Lavoisier shows that burning is caused by a reaction with oxygen. He shows that water is made from hydrogen and oxygen.

1803: John Dalton shows that elements are made of atoms.

1807: Humphry Davy uses electricity to split compounds into elements.

1860: Gustav Kirchhoff shows that elements release specific colors when they burn.

1868: Helium is discovered in the Sun's atmosphere. It is identified by its light.

1869: Dmitri Mendeleev develops a periodic table of elements.

1889: Svante Arrhenius shows that chemical reactions require a boost of energy to start.

1896: Henri Becquerel discovers radioactivity.

1898: Marie and Pierre Curie discover that radioactivity came from certain elements, such as thorium and radium.

1911: The Haber process turns nitrogen in the air into useful substances.

1913: Isotopes are discovered.

1940: Elements heavier than uranium are produced in laboratories. The first are neptunium and plutonium.

1985: Buckminsterfullerene is discovered as a new form of pure carbon.

2014: The periodic table has 118 entries.

GLOSSARY

atomic mass: A measure of how much matter is inside an atom.

atomic number: The number of protons in an atom.

charge: A property of particles that makes things positively or negatively charged.

compound: A substance made from a combination of two or more elements.

electron: A small subatomic particle that has a negative charge. Electrons are involved in making bonds between atoms.

element: A substance that cannot be broken down into any simpler ingredients.

energy: A property needed to alter the motion or state of matter.

mass: A measure of how much matter is in an object.

neutron: A subatomic particle found in the nucleus of most atoms. It has no charge.

nucleus: An atom's central core.

pressure: A measure of how much force is pushing against a particular area. Gases exert pressure on objects around them.

proton: A subatomic particle found in the nucleus of most atoms. It has a positive charge.

radioactivity: When an unstable atom breaks apart.

subatomic: Smaller than an atom.

FOR MORE INFORMATION

BOOKS

Clowes, Martin. *The Basics of Organic Chemistry*. New York: Rosen Publishing, 2014.

Cobb, Allan B. *The Basics of Chemistry*. New York: Rosen Publishing, 2014.

Green, Dan. *Scholastic Discover More: The Elements*. New York, NY: Scholastic Reference, 2012.

WEB SITES

Because of the changing nature of Internet links, Rosen Publishing has developed an online list of websites related to the subject of this book. This site is updated regularly. Please use this link to access this list:

http://www.rosenlinks.com/SCIB/Chem

INDEX